3 1526 03959401 2

GIRLS ALOUD

POSY EDWARDS

D1511683

INTRODUCTION

Breaking boundaries is what Girls Aloud are about. Over the years, the girls have taken the music industry by storm and transformed themselves from potential popstars to sassy divas, blazing a trail of number one anthems and blockbuster sell-out tours. The girls have had everthing the media can throw at them and still they come back stronger every year. In eight years, Girls Aloud have broken almost every record there is in the industry and done it with attitude, grace and style. And still the girls are here, standing tall, together and stronger than ever. Some would call it durability, we call it rockability!

SALES & AWARDS

20 consecutive top 10 singles
4 number one singles
6 platinum albums
6 million CD sales
1 Brit Award
6 Brit Award nominations

Nadine

Born: June 15, 1985

Hometown: Derry, but now lives in Los Angeles

Star sign: Gemini

Fave TV Shows: Any cooking programme

Never leaves home without: Moisturiser, toothbrush, hand cream and nail file

Fave Girls Aloud moment: 'When we did *Saturday Night Divas*. Chaka Khan and Celine Dion were on with us. It was great.'

Hates: Social politics and negativity

Fave Girls Aloud Video: *Sexy! No No No...*

Nadine's parents love their daughter's new hometown, LA, so much that they're thinking of moving over there to open an Irish bar. 'We want to serve the traditional food and have a good sing-song every night,' says Nadine's dad, Niall.

Kimberley nearly got the part of Maria on Coronation Street

Born: 20 November, 1981

Hometown: Bradford

Star sign: Scorpio

Loves: Her mum, performing and cooking

Hates: Weight obsession

Greatest fashion faux pas:
'A terrible perm when I was 13 or 14'

Kimberley

Never goes for night out without:
Credit card, cash, chewing gum, lip-gloss,
eyeliner and powder

To pass the time on tour she loves:
Baking with Sarah

Fave celebs she's met: Alicia Keys,
Denzel Washington

Cheryl

Born: 30 July, 1983

Hometown: Newcastle

Star sign: Leo

Hates: Liars and celebrity columnists

Fave holiday destination: Thailand

Fave musicians: Mary J. Blige, Alicia Keys

Phobias: Cotton wool. Eewww!

Fave food: Sushi

Favourite TV: Ricki Lake

Cheryl's rule of life is never have regrets, just learn from your mistakes.

Nicola

Born: 5 October, 1985

Hometown: Cheshire

Star sign: Libra

Loves: Liverpool FC

Fave labels: Chanel, Balenciaga, Miu Miu

Never goes for night out without: perfume, phone, credit card, house keys and make up

Fave holiday destination: St Tropez

The youngest of the group, Nicola was only 16 at the time of the audition and had just finished her GCSEs a few weeks before!

Sarah

Born: 17 November, 1981

Hometown: Berkshire

Star sign: Scorpio

Loves: Horse-riding, computer games and cooking

Hates: Disloyalty

Fave label: Topshop

Fave subjects at school: Home Economics and PE

Fave Girls Aloud Video: *Sound of the Underground*

Sarah was one of the celebrity bridesmaids for Jordan's wedding to Peter Andre!

POPSTARS

In the summer of 2002, before anybody had even heard of *The X Factor*, Saturday nights were all about gathering round the telly to watch *Popstars: The Rivals*. Much like the reality music shows we know and love now, the format involved young hopefuls from across the country singing their hearts out under the scrutiny of judges and the general public. The format involved ten girls and ten boys in competition to form a rival boy and girl band with each final group releasing singles to reach the Christmas number one spot. Pretty scary stuff, even for the super confident girls we see before us today.

AUDITIONS

It's amazing to think that at one stage all the girls were just young hopefuls with an audition number on a sticker and their dreams. As Kimberley says, 'I'd done lots of auditions but this one was really scary and I didn't know if I was going to be able to hold my nerve.'

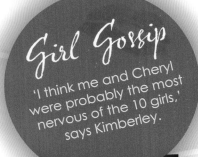

Girl Gossip

'I think me and Cheryl were probably the most nervous of the 10 girls,' says Kimberley.

EARLY NERVES

After weeks of more auditions and deliberations amongst the judges, our five girls were told that they'd made it to the final ten. All the girls would be moving away from their homes, most for the first time, to start an adventure that would shape their lives. The girls found the whole experience of doing the show hard and extremely tiring. 'It was mentally draining,' says Nadine. 'I just kept getting ill and coming out in cold sores with stress.'

Sarah agrees, 'the live shows were awful. I can't say there was one performance on that programme where I sang my best.'

Girl Gossip

As ever Cheryl had the full support of her beloved Newcastle. At one stage during *Popstars: The Rivals*, the Tyne Bridge was draped in a 40 foot 'Vote for Cheryl' banner!

17

EVICTION SCARES

Still the girls stuck at it and, as the weeks and performances went on, the makings of Girls Aloud began. But not without the odd close shave. It seems funny to think of it now but arguably the biggest star of the band, Cheryl, came very close to being voted off the show, falling into the final two on a number of occasions. Strong as ever, she persevered and made it through, gaining the judges backing whenever she came close to the end.

Facing eviction from the competition was tough for everyone, not only were dreams and careers being destroyed but also friendships were being lost. 'I was in the bottom three with Cheryl and Aimee in week three,' says Kimberley, 'and when it came down to the two of them it was just awful. All of us loved both of them and it was getting to the point we were all so close that we didn't want anybody to go.'

Girl Gossip

When starting out, the girls dreamed of emulating their heroes, the Spice Girls, with Cheryl saying: 'we would love to have the same success as the Spice Girls. They really made it. They paved the way for girl groups and we'd love to think this is our time now.'

A BAND IS BORN

Finally, it all came down to one night when the band was revealed. All five of the girls whooped and hollered when their names were called out. But getting into the band wasn't enough. Sure they had their record deal but to go one step further and win the competition and beat the boys to the Christmas number one would be the real icing on the cake.

Girl Gossip

'To be Christmas number one was more than we ever expected, it was an exhausting few weeks but we couldn't stop screaming! It was the perfect present.' says Cheryl.

One True Voice, backed by Pete Waterman, had won the boys section of the competition and were set to release a double A-side single including a cover of the Bee Gees' *Sacred Trust* and original track *Long After You've Gone*. The girls, backed by Louis Walsh, went with a cover of East 17's *Stay Another Day* and *Sound of the Underground*. Christmas 2002 was all about the battle of the bands and was taken very seriously by the public, the producers and the boys. But the girls thought One True Voice were certainties to win. 'We thought all the girls would buy their single and we weren't going to get number one, so we were just having a laugh.'

Of course, the boys didn't have a hope against Girls Aloud and *Sound of the Underground* stormed its way to number one, and stayed there for four weeks, going platinum with 600,000 copies sold. Girls Aloud had arrived.

MAKING IT

With *Popstars: The Rivals* behind them, the pressure was on for Girls Aloud to stay in the limelight and establish themselves. The girls went straight to work on a debut album and were soon on television every week performing their new material. Nicola remembers it as a wildly exciting time: 'we'd all grown up watching CD:UK every Saturday morning and it was totally our thing. Then we got in the band and we were there almost every week and we were so excited about it… We were on with people like Mary J. Blige and Justin Timberlake but we didn't need the big names to make it feel like, wow!'

ALBUMS AND VIDEOS

With the massive success of their first single, the music world waited in eager anticipation for more hits from Girls Aloud and the new band didn't disappoint with their debut album *Sound of the Underground* going gold and selling 100,000 copies within months, and reaching number two in the charts! More singles followed in the form of *Life Got Cold* about which Cheryl says, 'we just wanted a really beautiful ballad that shows off all our voices, and just to show… that we can actually sing.'

Movie success soon followed suit as the girls were asked to record the lead single, *Jump*, for Richard Curtis's (of *Four Weddings and a Funeral* and *Notting Hill* fame) latest flick, *Love Actually*. All the girls claim that *Jump* was a big turning point. '*Jump* went down really well,' says Nadine. 'People loved the fun side of it. We loved it. It was all a bit dark before and we were fun young girls so *Jump* was kind of where we wanted to go.' A flurry of red carpet movie premieres followed, and with their hit singles making it in blockbuster movies, Girls Aloud were part of the A-list crowd now.

Girl Gossip

Girls Aloud were the first band to get to Christmas number one with a debut single, and it's the quickest any band has gone from being formed to having a number one.

SOUND OF THE UNDERGROUND

Who could not love their debut album *Sound of the Underground*. For the girls it's very dear to their heart, being their first piece of work. The girls think of the album as 'edgy' and 'fresh' with other hit singles such as *Life Got Cold* and *Jump* all causing a storm.

Girl Gossip

One of the tracks on *Sound of the Underground*, Girls Allowed, was written for the group by ex-Westlife star Bryan McFadden.

WHAT WILL THE NEIGHBOURS SAY?

Released in November 2004 with singles such as *The Show*, *Love Machine*, *I'll Stand by You* and *Wake Me Up*, *What Will the Neighbours Say* is a classic and really starts to show the girls developing their own sound. But the recording of the album wasn't without problems, especially the hit single *Love Machine*, which was hated by all the girls at the start. 'Everyone knows *Love Machine*', says Sarah. 'It's instantly recognisable, but we all hated it at first. We thought it was cheesy… The more we heard it the more it grew on us.'

'It turned to be one of our favourite songs and one of our favourite videos as well,' says Kimberley of *Love Machine*.

CHEMISTRY

Preceded by the singles *Long Hot Summer* and *Biology*, their third album, *Chemistry*, was released in December 2005. Despite being the band's lowest charting album to date, it still went platinum and contains singles that signified the band's acceptance into the music establishment. According to Cheryl 'when *Biology* came out we started accepting ourselves and thinking, you know what, we do make good pop songs.'

Kimberley agrees: 'when we did the *Chemistry* album it was quite a turning point for us. It's one of my favourite albums. I felt like every song had a totally different vibe.'

THE SOUND OF GIRLS ALOUD

Girls Aloud released their greatest hits anthology in 2006, just four years after forming. The album included their twelve singles released to date and three new songs. Two of the songs, *Something Kinda Ooooh* and *I Think We're Alone Now* were released as singles and recorded last minute to help promote the album. 'I'm talking last minute' says Nicola. 'Just as the album was about to go and suddenly we had a song.'

TANGLED UP

Released in 2007 *Tangled Up* entered the UK album chart at number four. It was preceded by the lead single *Sexy! No No No...*, many of the girls' favourite song to date. 'I loved the fierce energy of *Sexy! No No No...*' says Nadine. 'And I really like the video.' Nicola agrees, 'I still love the video for *Sexy! No No No...* because it's quirky and different and the movements were quite angular, and that really suited me.'

The album is generally seen as more upbeat than a lot of their other work but the girls still felt there's even more room to evolve. 'I still think we have room to grow,' said Kimberley.

'*Tangled Up* has more of a dance vibe, but by the time we do the next album it will be different again.'

OUT OF CONTROL

The group's nineteenth single, *The Promise*, was released in October 2008, and went straight in the charts at number one. The girls' fifth studio album – which was released on 2 November with singles such as *The Loving Kind* and *Untouchable* – was released in 2009 to a fantastic reception. This album resulted in the girls getting their highest acclaim, winning a Brit Award for *The Promise*, beating artists such as Coldplay, Leona Lewis and Duffy. About time too!

Girl Gossip

The girls teamed up with another UK girl band, Sugababes, to record number one hit Walk This Way for Comic Relief 2007.

GIRLS TODAY

As with any group of girls, rumours of fall-outs have been rife since the band formed. But as always, things said in the press about the girls couldn't be further from the truth, after all not many successful pop groups would be able to last as long as they have – unless they got along with each other.

As Kimberley says, 'looking in from the outside you'd probably expect there to be fireworks constantly between five girls because we all have pretty strong opinions, but I think nine times out of ten we've all had the same vision for the group and we know to leave our differences in personality aside.'

The girls have been on such an incredible journey they're tighter now than ever. 'We have been through so much together. None of us are from London and we're living away from our friends and family. We only have each other and that's what has made us so tight - that's why we have to remain as a five'.

Cheryl agrees saying, 'most importantly nobody is allowed to get too big for their boots, no matter how famous they become. 'If any of us got above our station the others would soon stamp it out,' says Nadine.

LOVE

Between them, when it comes to love, the girls have seen it all – fairytale romances, childhood sweethearts, fleeting crushes and earth-shattering heartbreak are all part of the Girls Aloud story in love.

Girl Gossip

During the filming of the theme to *St Trinians*, the girls were given a trailer each but because they were not used to such privileges, they all piled into Cheryl's together!

SARAH IN LOVE

Sarah definitely digs the footballer connection having been rumoured to have had a relationship with Calum Best (son of George Best). She also had an on-off relationship with fellow *Popstars: The Rivals* contestant Mikey Green (now of the boy band Phixx) for a few years.

But it seems as if she's settled down these days, with DJ boyfriend, Tommy Crane, with whom she now lives. 'With Tommy I just felt like he ticked all the boxes… Tommy's really only my third long-term relationship and it did feel different when we got together. What struck me about him is he's just so funny and happy and chirpy all the time.'

Sarah is aware that she's been naïve in the past when it comes to men and is now more cautious: 'I am so wary about getting involved with someone again because it's horrible when it all comes to an end. Before, I used to go out with people and hear wedding bells straight away, but now it's different. I take my relationships seriously.' And it looks like things are getting 'serious' with Tommy: 'I'm hoping to settle down with Tommy and have marriage and kids.' Maybe we'll be having another Girls Aloud wedding sooner than we think!

NICOLA IN LOVE

When Nicola embarked on her Girls Aloud journey she was already in a relationship with her childhood sweetheart, Carl Egerton, with whom she'd been going out since the age of 16. The relationship went on for five years and Nicola used to even refer to him as 'the sixth band member'. But sadly the pressures of stardom and success soon got to the couple and they broke up in 2006. Still Nicola holds a place for Carl in her heart, saying 'I will always care for him, he was my first love.'

Nicola is now single and very happy: 'Right now men aren't even coming into my mind. I don't even want to think about them. I want to be single.' Not to say Nicola wants to be alone forever, though. Eventually she would like to find love and have the happy ending: 'I want to fall in love and get married and have children. Just not right now.'

CHERYL IN LOVE

Not since Posh and Becks has there been such a high profile footballer/popstar wedding. Ashley proposed to Cheryl on a romantic holiday in Dubai before giving Cheryl the fairytale wedding she'd always dreamed of. Despite having a troubled relationship, Cheryl always managed to get through the tough times largely thanks to the support from the girls in the band.

Cheryl has learned a lot from her troubled times with Ashley: 'Things are sent to test you and I would hate to be an untested person. I'm glad I've had the ups and downs. I can't hurt any more than I've been hurt, I can't cry anymore than I've cried. I've been to the highest highs and the lowest lows, so one day I'm going to find my middle ground and be happy.'

This year, Cheryl was linked with co-performer and Black Eyed Peas front man, Will.i.am. But when asked if the two performers were an item Cheryl replied 'I would work with Will for the rest of my life if I could. He's everything you would want from a producer, and also a person. He's a lovely person... I'd work with him every day if I could,' but there wasn't any suggestion of anything more than just friendship.

KIMBERLEY IN LOVE

When Kimberley joined the band she was dating footballer Martin Pemberton. But as the band grew the relationship strained and the pair soon split on amicable terms. 'We hardly saw each other to be fair,' says Kimberley. 'We were both really busy with work and that meant when we saw each other we took it out on each other. We thought it best to cut our losses and go our separate ways. We are still on speaking terms.'

In 2004 Kimberley finally found true love with Triple 8 singer Justin Scott and while the relationship doesn't command the same press attention as her band mates, Kimberley is blissfully happy with her man.

'Justin and I are really happy. We're definitely moving in the right direction. He gets on well with all my family so if we do marry, it would be a lovely set-up.'

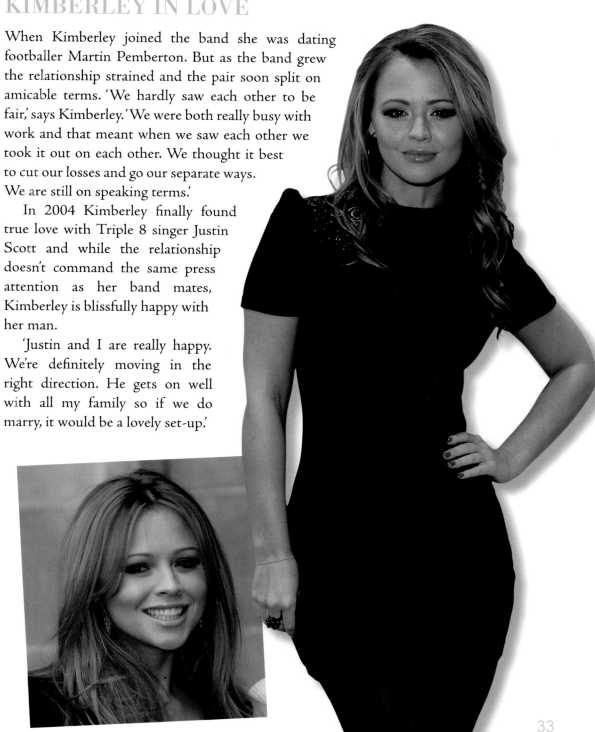

Girl Gossip

Nadine says 'it's hard being in a girlband but if you want to take the time out and work at a relationship it can work.'

NADINE IN LOVE

Living stateside in LA has meant that Nadine has been finding love in the form of hunky Americans of late. Her most high-profile relationship has been with *Desperate Housewives* heartthrob, Jesse Metcalfe.

From the first time they met, the Hollywood star was wowed by the small town girl from Derry. 'I was struck by the way she played it so cool,' says Jesse. 'The way she carries herself – she's definitely a lady. She has a lot of respect for herself. Right after the first night we hung out, I knew I wanted to spend more time with her.'

The pair had a tricky on-off relationship, and things eventually ended. The main problems arose from their age difference according to Nadine. 'I was 20 when I met him… he was 28 and wanted to settle down… We were two people wanting different things and that made it really difficult to find somewhere in between.'

Nadine has since moved on to a new relationship with American Football star Jason Bell but she insists that she's still not ready for marriage. 'I would laugh if I saw myself in a wedding dress. I feel too young, as strange as it sounds. I just don't think I'm mature enough to do that at the minute,' says Nadine. 'But is Jason the most incredible man I've met? Of course - by a mile… I don't have an idea for the perfect wedding, I'm just sure that when the time comes it'll be all right. The actual wedding day is not that important, it's all about making sure you're with the right person.'

THE LOOK

The girls have been known to wear anything and everything from football shirts to Fendi, but no matter what they always have that wow factor. Over the years their look has matured from bubble-gum pop princess to gorgeous and elegant divas.

For Sarah, how you feel and confidence are more important than your size or what you're wearing: 'You don't have to be super skinny, but if you have the right attitude, other people will believe in that as well.'

GIRLS TOP BEAUTY AND STYLE SECRETS

Kimberley: 'When it's all like "curvy Kimberley" it could go either way. But luckily I'm glad I look the way I do!'

Cheryl: 'I just make sure my face is clean and that I'm cleansed and moisturised before I go to bed.'

Nicola: 'I've got really sensitive skin so anything too perfumed or harsh makes it break out. I use Garnier at the moment and I just keep things simple.'

Nadine: 'I always drink water because you just know it's good for you and I've always liked healthy food.'

Sarah: 'I like going to the gym and I go through phases where I do a lot of working out.'

Girl Gossip

Cheryl on body art 'I absolutely love my tattoos. The girls and I decided that the next time Girls Aloud have a No. 1, we'll all get one done. I want us to get something that only makes sense if we all stand in line, though!'

Girl Gossip

Girls Aloud were the last act ever to be seen on Top of the Pops.

39

THE FUTURE IS BRIGHT

With so much talent amongst them all it only makes sense that the girls should explore what they've got to offer individually. Reality shows, musicals and the movies are all on the cards for the girls as they look to the future.

Girl Gossip

Cheryl on Simon Cowell:
'People think Simon's harsh
and nasty, but he's not, not
one bit. He's got a heart
of gold. He's real, very
charismatic, and he's
a pleasure to
work with.'

CHERYL

Cheryl has become even more famous for being a judge on *The X Factor*. Having been through *Popstars: The Rivals* she is the most compassionate and caring of all the judges, and as a result the public love her. The manner in which she brought fellow Geordie Joe McElderry under her wing and treated him as a younger brother endeared her to the nation.

Cheryl now has a booming solo career, partly in thanks to her collaboration with Will.i.am in *Heartbreaker*. Her resulting album, *3 Words*, and debut solo single 'Fight For This Love' both charted at number one. Her new album is rumoured to be out in late 2010 and there are rumours of collaborations with Gary Barlow!

SARAH

Sarah is also planning solo projects, and looking at going down a Gaga route:

'I'm so excited about going into the studio,' says Sara. 'I haven't completely settled on what kind of music I'm going to make yet, but I would love it to be something like Lady Gaga. She is the new Madonna as far as I'm concerned. When we saw her at the O2 a couple of weeks ago I was blown away.'

Sarah's also interested in getting into acting 'I love thrillers. I'd love to do something quite psychological, paranormal. I'm a bit sinister like that but I also love comedy as well, I love a good comedy.'

KIMBERLEY

Aside from the band, Kimberley does some modelling and is heavily involved in charity work. But looking to the future, Kimberley is keen to tread the boards of the West End: 'doing musicals might be something I could think about way in the future.'

Sarah agrees, saying 'I think Kimberley would be amazing at musicals actually. She loves musicals, she knows every single one inside out.'

NICOLA

Nicola's sideline projects involve her make-up line, Dainty Doll, and being the new face of Vivienne Westwood. But when it comes to the immediate future, all her focus is concentrated on the band, which she always feels lucky to be a part of. 'We still pinch ourselves and know that the career and opportunities we have are not something we will ever take for granted.' But she's confident she could make a go of anything if the band broke up tomorrow. 'I'm a very ambitious person, very career minded, and I'll try my hand at whatever comes my way.'

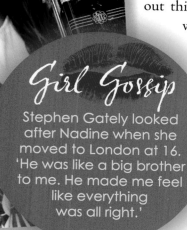

NADINE

Nadine is just embarking on solo projects having recorded an as yet unreleased track with Jay Sean. Her first solo album is due out this year, plus she's already performed with other groups, having sung with Boyzone on their TV tribute to the late Stephen Gately. 'It was strange standing in his place,' says Nadine on singing with Boyzone. 'And the lads joked, "Don't sing the song too good or Stephen will be cursing you from above."'

Girl Gossip

Stephen Gately looked after Nadine when she moved to London at 16. 'He was like a big brother to me. He made me feel like everything was all right.'

TOGETHER FOREVER?

With all their successful solo projects, fans must wonder how much longer will the girls be able to stay together? But Sarah thinks the solo projects are a good thing for the band: 'I think having space from each other is a good thing. People were in each other's faces all the time. It's good to have a break so we can see our own friends, who have been neglected for the seven years we've been together.' But of the future Sarah says, 'I don't know what the future is for the band. We'll just have to re-evaluate when the time comes. It's hard to know.'

For the moment Cheryl is confident that they'll have plenty more albums to come in the future: 'There are three albums just sitting there waiting to do – it just hasn't been put into place yet.' So here's hoping to at least three more albums and many more years of Girls Aloud.

PICTURE CREDITS

All pictures courtesy of Getty Images.

ACKNOWLEDGEMENTS

Posy Edwards would like to Guyan Mitra, Jane Sturrock, Nicola Crossley, Helen Ewing, James Martindale, and Rich Carr.

Copyright © Posy Edwards 2010

The right of Posy Edwards to be identified as
the author of this work has been asserted in accordance with the
Copyright, Designs and Patents Act 1988.

First published in hardback in Great Britain in 2010 by
Orion Books an imprint of the Orion Publishing Group Ltd
Orion House, 5 Upper St Martin's Lane, London WC2H 9EA
An Hachette UK Company

10 9 8 7 6 5 4 3 2 1

All rights reserved. Apart from any use permitted under UK copyright
law, this publication may only be reproduced, stored or transmitted,
in any form, or by any means, with prior permission in writing of the
publishers or, in the case of reprographic production, in accordance
with the terms of licences issued by the Copyright Licensing Agency.

A CIP catalogue record for this book is available from the British
Library.

ISBN: 978 1 4091 2313 2

Designed by www.carrstudio.co.uk
Printed in Spain by Cayfosa

The Orion Publishing Group's policy is to use papers that are natural,
renewable and recyclable and made from wood grown in sustainable
forests. The logging and manufacturing processes are expected to
conform to the environmental regulations of the country of origin.

Every effort has been made to fulfil requirements with regard to
reproducing copyright material. The author and publisher will be glad
to rectify any omissions at the earliest opportunity.
www.orionbooks.co.uk